CAREERS IN

AUTOMOTIVE DESIGN

CHOOSING A CAREER CAN SEEM A daunting task. Naturally, you want to get it right. Don't let the importance of this decision intimidate you, however. Do just the opposite. Use its importance to bolster your enthusiasm for doing the research to help you make the right choice. The fact that you are taking the time to read this report is a good sign.

Start by considering what you like to do. This isn't the only question you should ask yourself when starting your career search, but it's definitely the most important one. Money, work environment and your own natural aptitudes are all important, but nothing is worse than choosing a career based on something other than personal satisfaction. Determine what you would be happy to do for free, and then figure out how to get paid for it.

Cars inspire more emotion than any other manufactured product ever made. In fact, it's easy to forget that they are, indeed, manufactured products. Cars are larger and more complicated than, say, can openers, but they are made out of the same materials and in similar factory environments.

Automobiles inspire so many emotions because they embody and express those emotions. For most people, their car is the second-most expensive thing they own, after only their home. Cars are an outward reflection of income and status, taste and personality. Cars are the main manifestation of the personal freedom of movement that we take for granted. For most of human history, most people never ventured more than a few miles from the place where they were born, making the ability to go anywhere at any time a powerful self-esteem builder. Cars are fun to drive. They enable people to get to work and pursue their ambitions.

Automotive designers are the people who add the emotional component to the pieces of metal and leather assembled by the mechanical engineers who design the engines and associated running gear that most people never see. In fact, most people choose cars based on a combination of looks and price, with performance coming in a distant third place. Engineers and marketing executives play roles in taking ideas off the drawing board and bringing them to life, but designers are the automotive professionals who make cars appeal to the people who will buy them, and drive them.

WHAT TO DO FIRST

THERE ARE MANY WAYS FOR YOU TO get started on your career in automotive design. In school, take classes in auto shop and art. Automotive designers generally earn degrees in industrial design, a discipline which blends elements of engineering and art in order to give students the tools necessary to design objects that are practical as well as visually appealing. Automotive designers may not have a hand in designing suspension systems, for example, but they have to know enough about how they work to make sure that their designs will complement the engineering. It's not just about curvy lines and alluring chrome. Before it can be stylist, automotive design has to serve the engineering that makes the car go, and comfortable and practical for the people who will drive the car. Take as many classes in auto shop and art as you possibly can.

Then apply what you learn on your own car. Most automotive designers are basically car buffs at heart who managed to make their passion their profession. Paint your car. Redesign the interior. Modify the engine. Make your car a reflection of your creativity. This is essentially what you will be doing for a living and you'll learn by doing it on your own time. Be bold. Take risks. You can always undo bad decisions later. You'll learn a little more every time you do.

There is no better, faster way to learn about a profession or industry than by reading the trade journals devoted to it. Some prominent titles include *AutoWeek, Car and Driver, Classic and Sportscar, Motor Trend, Classic Motorsports, Hemmings Motor News, Hot Rod, Practical Classics*. There are also dozens of small-circulation titles devoted to specific brands, or "marques." Find a few that you like and read them regularly.

HISTORY OF THE CAREER

THE EARLIEST CARS WERE MOSTLY spindly contraptions based on the horse-drawn carriages that preceded them. They were not designed as cars, but rather as evolutions of existing carriages. They were also object lessons in the most important rule of industrial design, which says that form must follow function. An industrial product must work before any thought can be put into making it stylish or attractive. The earliest cars barely worked, requiring decades of refinement before anybody started to worry about what they looked like.

Introduced in 1908, the Ford Model T was the car that forced design to become a major consideration when building cars. The Model T was a very simple car itself, featuring a cloth roof, wooden-spoke wheels and a minimal body. Henry Ford, whose company produced the car, once joked that customers could have the car in any color they wanted "as long as it's black." The car was utilitarian, inexpensive and wildly successful.

The Model T revolutionized automotive design by quickly filling a market that hadn't even existed a few years before. By the mid-1920s most middle-class households in the United States had a car, and most of them were Model Ts or very similar cars from other companies.

Auto manufacturers realized they had to find ways to entice consumers to buy new cars every few years. They achieved this goal by offering new designs. This process helped to sell cars in two ways. First, it peaked consumers' interest by offering flashy new styles that caught attention. Second, the new styles necessarily made the old styles look unfashionable. Creative design inspired consumers to get rid of their old cars as much as it inspired them to buy new ones. This method became known as "planned obsolescence," or designing new products simply to replace old products even if the old products were still up to the job. A very smooth move on the part of the car companies and one immediately copied by other manufacturers.

By the 1930s most automobiles were enclosed and made of steel. The cloth roofs and wooden bodies of the early years were long gone, clinging on in only a few limited-production cars. Convertibles became the exception rather than the norm. Enclosed cars were safer, lighter and more secure, all design issues that hadn't been considered in earlier years when emphasis was almost entirely on mechanical reliability. The cars of the 1930s were streamlined, taking their cues from the impressive railroad locomotives that were still the favored means of long-distance travel.

Automotive design was interrupted by World War II. From early 1942 through 1945 all American auto plants were reconfigured for wartime production. Tanks, planes and military vehicles rolled off the assembly lines in huge numbers, making American industrial might a major factor in winning the war. Do a little research and you will find that there are no American cars with the 1942 to 1945 model years, aside from a handful of 1942 models sold in late 1941. Auto production resumed in 1946 with what amounted to rehashes of 1942 models that had never made it into production. It took years for American society and industry to revert to normal after the war, and automotive design took no major strides until the 1950s.

And what strides they were! No era in automotive design screams louder than the 1950s. Cars sported two-tone pastel paint jobs, acres of chrome, hood ornaments a foot long and tailfins that made the cars look like they were going fast even when they were standing still. Planned obsolescence consisted of annual styling tweaks to cars that remained mechanically unaltered for a decade at a time. A ripple here, a strake there and a couple of new splashes of chrome, and instantly everybody who bought last year's model wanted the new model. Some cars were positively glorious in their wretched excess, such as the 1959 Cadillac Eldorado, which claimed the tallest-ever tailfins at 48 inches high. The Eldorado looks overwrought today, but some cars from the era have aged very well. The perfectly proportioned tailfin on the 1957 Chevrolet Bel Air remains one of the hallmarks of outstanding industrial design. Other cars were disasters, and none more so than the Ford Edsel. Named for founder Henry Ford's son, the Edsel featured an enormous, ovular grille that was instantly compared to a horsecollar or, even worse, a toilet seat. The Edsel was such a disaster in terms of design and marketing – Ford lost hundreds of millions of dollars on it – that the name "Edsel" became a synonym for product failure. Look up a photo of one. What do you think?

By the early 1960s American automobiles had taken on new inspiration in the form of the jet aircraft that defined the Cold War era. Bodies trimmed down, became long and lean and featured touches redolent of aircraft, including round taillights that looked like jet engines and sleek windshields that looked like aircraft canopies. The Ford Thunderbird from 1961 to 1963, for example, is a car that wants to take flight. In late 1964 Ford introduced the Mustang, the mid-sized sporty car that became the first of what would be known as "pony cars." The end of the decade saw the arrival of the muscle car. The Pontiac GTO, Chevrolet Camaro, Dodge

Charger and Challenger, and the American Motors Javelin all featured huge engines, wide tires and streamlined bodies. They looked and sounded as aggressive as they were.

The next major influence in automotive design was legal rather than emotional. In 1974 the federal government issued a raft of safety and environmental regulations that forever changed the ways in which auto designers did their business. Early efforts to adapt to these restrictions went badly, as engineers tried to reduce pollution and enhance the fuel economy of old engine designs, and designers tried to add flair to bodies that now needed to be designed with crumple zones to absorb crash impact, among other considerations. American auto design, inside and out, didn't really recover until the 1990s. Search the Internet for American cars from the late 1970s and all of the 1980s. Can you find any that are considered "classic?"

Foreign designs also influenced American automotive design during this era. After World War II the only foreign cars readily available in the United States were small sports cars, mostly from the United Kingdom, and cheap economy cars like the Volkswagen Beetle, from Germany. By the 1970s major foreign manufacturers were exporting a wide range of cars into the United States, mostly from Germany and Japan, the latter a newcomer to the American market. Huge, gas-guzzling American cars that had to be replaced every few years were quickly challenged by the foreign arrivals, which tended to be smaller, more economical and more reliable. When the first oil shortage resulted in spiking gas prices in the early 1970s, the glorious excesses of the past were no longer so attractive to consumers.

The modern American auto market includes foreign and domestic brands competing side-by-side in every category, from sports cars to sport-utility vehicles to luxury cars. Design has become more subtle than ever, with automotive designers working their magic inside and out in ways that consumers may not even consciously notice. The technological challenges of the first wave of federal regulations have been largely overcome, resulting in cars that are once again stylish to look at and exciting to drive. Designers still have their fair share of hits and misses. The Pontiac Aztek sport-utility vehicle, released in

2001, was actually singled out in one poll as the ugliest car of all time, beating even the dreadful Edsel. On the other hand, the reimagined Dodge Challenger, which hit the market in 2008 as an updated version of the inspired 1970 design, is generally regarded as way-cool in a way that only a muscle car can be.

WHERE YOU WILL WORK

DETROIT IS KNOWN AS THE MOTOR CITY FOR A REASON. The Big Three American auto manufacturers, General Motors, Ford and Chrysler, are all headquartered in the city and its suburbs. Most of the American brands of the past made their home in Detroit too, like Packard, Studebaker, Hudson, Nash and the tiny Detroit Electric, a manufacturer several decades ahead of its time that went out of business in 1939. Approximately 70 percent of the economic activity of the Detroit metropolitan area is in some way dependent upon the auto industry. If your goal is to make it to the top of the auto design profession, to put your stamp on entire cars that will roll off assembly lines and onto highways around the world, you will probably head to Detroit someday. You may even choose to spend your entire career there.

Not that Detroit is the only place to carve out a career. Detroit is where American cars come together, but the bits and pieces that comprise them come from all over. The Big Three all maintain elaborate networks of suppliers and contractors around the United States and all over the world. If a manufacturer needs, for example, a side-view mirror for a new car it may solicit designs from several contractors and choose one to put into production. The companies that do this kind of design work are not necessarily located in Detroit. They can be found in major metropolitan areas around the country.

The automobile industry is a global concern. General Motors owns part of Japanese brand Suzuki, for example, and all of the ostensibly German car company Opel. Italian automotive giant Fiat owns a third of Chrysler, giving Chrysler links to legendary Italian manufacturers like Lancia, Alfa Romeo, Maserati and Ferrari. Ford owns small stakes in British firm Aston Martin and Japanese manufacturer Mazda. Auto companies routinely leverage expertise within their organizations by moving people around from one brand to another. If you make it to the top of the Chrysler design hierarchy, for example, you could find yourself working for Ferrari in Italy for a few years.

WORK DUTIES

Interior Designer

Most people tend not to think about automotive interiors very much. Exteriors catch the eye when a car is glimpsed on the street or in most advertisements. Interiors come in cloth or leather, black or beige. Almost nobody chooses a car based on its interior styling. But that doesn't mean that interior design isn't important.

Interiors contribute greatly to overall automotive design and presence. Properly executed interiors complement the exterior and make passengers feel like they're riding in the stylish car they got into, even though they can't see the exterior styling from the inside. Interiors also have a psychological effect that most people don't even notice, whether it's the sense of power that comes with the purposeful interior of a powerful sports car or the feeling of thrift designed into the interior of an economy car. Automotive interior designers have to keep the car's overall purpose in mind during the design process.

Automotive interior design is all about the details. While exterior designers concentrate on adding detail to surfaces that are mostly broad and purposeful, interior designers have to accommodate thousands of details right from the beginning. Knobs, switches, handles, dials, gauges, LCD displays, vents, stalks, doors, lids, armrests, seatbelts, floor mats, map pockets, sun visors, makeup mirrors, dashboards, rear decks, headliners, pillars and speakers are just some of the bits and pieces that interior designers need to keep in mind while designing automotive interiors. Some of these items already exist and have been used in other models, but others have to be designed from scratch for a particular car. Interiors must also be designed with human occupancy in mind, meaning designers have to make sure everybody has enough headroom and legroom, as well as enough room to haul some cargo. Automotive interior design is a very precise, detail-oriented profession.

In order to make these details come to life, automotive interior designers have a bewildering array of materials to choose from. Many of the world's most advanced fabrics, plastics and composites were developed primarily for use in automotive interiors. Cars have to be able to withstand daily abuse that an ordinary piece of furniture could never overcome. Kids, pets, food and beverage spills, trips to hardware stores that result in odd things being placed in the car, like 100 pounds of potting soil or half-a-dozen eight-foot boards. Automotive interiors are designed to be durable and easy to clean, in addition to being attractive complements to their exteriors.

Exterior Designer

When most people think of automotive design they think of the alluring curves and swoopy contours that are the hallmark of well-designed automotive exteriors. There's no denying that exterior designers are the superstars of automotive design. Exteriors are what sell cars. They're what give them individuality and style. Exteriors make statements about their owners and where they fall in the socioeconomic scheme of things. Exteriors also play important roles in a car's performance. Exteriors are what people remember.

Exteriors are so important to automotive design that many of the concept cars that debut at auto shows around the world are nothing more than an empty shell resting on a phony chassis. Manufacturers gauge reaction to the new shape by asking the people who attend the shows what they think of it. Since most of the people who attend auto shows are in the business or in the motoring press, their opinions are vitally important. If the new shape gets an enthusiastic response, the manufacturer may decide to finish the project.

Exterior designers have to work closely with engineers and marketing professionals during the design process. Designers are usually given free reign to design whatever they fancy because creativity tends to flow more enthusiastically when it is unconstrained by practical concerns. It is always better to make a fanciful design practical than to make a practical design fanciful. Once the designer has determined the general direction of the project, the design and engineering teams can make compromises on the details.

The same process defines the relationship between designers and marketing analysts. A major manufacturer may use the same styling hallmarks in three different ways in order to appeal to three different target markets, for example. The marketing analysts may seize upon a distinctive combination of roof line and fender flares, say, and decide that these styling fillips will be hallmarks of the brand for the next few years. They will then work with the designer to devise three cars that use that combination to fill three market niches: a short-wheelbase version with two doors, a tall roof and a four-cylinder engine to target buyers looking for an economy car; a long-wheelbase version with four doors, a tall roof and a six-cylinder engine for buyers who need a family car; and a low-slung, short-wheelbase version with an eight-cylinder engine, a streamlined roof and aggressive fender flares for the high-performance buyer. This application of marketing research is also why it's easy to tell a Chrysler from a Ford even at a distance. Designers rarely get to build exactly whatever they want. They are the artistic minds who bring together the practical needs of the engineers and the market analysts into a package that people will want to buy.

Automotive exterior design is the most competitive arena of the automotive design profession. Many designers enter the profession with bachelor's degrees and portfolios filled with promise, but only a small number make it to the top. Along the way, most automotive designers find comfortable paths designing components, working as consultants or moving sideways into a related speciality within the larger profession of industrial design.

Design Executive

Very senior designers become the executives in charge of the design departments at their companies. There are only a few design executives at the very top at any given time. The careerists who make it to this level of the profession have worked very hard, and have become very successful.

Most design executives have titles like "executive vice president in charge of design," or something similar. By the time they get to this level they have spent several decades in the business, probably with the same company. They may have worked on all of the company's brands and probably on a few of the company's subsidiaries. They know everything there is to know about their company's recent design history and how those designs have fared in the market.

Design executives may do very little actual design. As with all executive positions, their job is to pull together the teams of designers needed to bring a car from the drawing board to the assembly line. They are leaders, first and foremost. Their extensive design experience helps them to put together people with the right skills and temperaments to get the job done.

Component Designer

Many automotive designers specialize in designing components to fit into an overall design. Bumpers, side-view mirrors, door handles, gas caps, grilles, headlights and numerous other details are almost always designed separately from the overall exterior design. The exterior designer may sketch these details into the larger design, thereby setting the direction to be taken by the component designers, but it's usually up to the component designers to figure out the details and complete finished products.

Not all component designers work for auto companies. Many work for smaller suppliers and manufacturers of accessories. Many of the components in a typical car are stock items purchased by auto manufacturers and are not designed in-house for a particular model. Other accessories are available as options or as aftermarket add-ons.

There's no point in designing a seat for a sports car, for example, when a company called Recaro already has the most recognized name in the market for racing seats. All three major American manufacturers offer Recaro seats as optional equipment on their high-end performance cars. The same goes for Brembo brakes, Bilstein shock absorbers and a host of other high-end components sold by auto manufacturers but designed and made by an outside source.

AUTOMOTIVE DESIGN PROS TELL THEIR OWN STORIES

I Am an Interior Designer

"When I tell people I'm an interior designer they always ask me for advice on decorating their homes. That's not my thing, I tell them. I design the interiors of their cars, where most people spend several hours per day in but never think about.

It's really pretty amazing that car interiors don't get more of the glory than they do. We pay hefty premiums for the optional interiors, with leather upholstery and wood trim, but we tend to ignore them once we are sitting in them. It's exteriors that grab our attention when we're walking through the showroom.

How well a car works for you and your family has little to do with how it looks on the outside. Kids don't spill milkshakes on the hood. Nobody stores change for the tollbooth on the roof. Trunks don't provide lumbar support. People buy their cars based largely upon how they look on the outside, but they grow to like or dislike them based on how well they perform once you're sitting in them.

Like most automotive designers I started my career dreaming about designing flashy exteriors. Along the way I was assigned to a few interior design teams and decided that I really liked it. I can't even begin to tell you how many details have to be considered when designing an automotive interior. We use literally thousands of data points to craft functional, attractive interiors that will withstand the rigors of day-to-day use. We choose from among hundreds of materials to achieve our goals. In fact, far more different kinds of materials go into automotive interiors than exteriors.

Interiors have to be designed with real people and their needs in mind. I once served on a team that designed an armrest with a storage bin that wasn't quite wide enough to accommodate a CD. It's not like there was some other engineering consideration that dictated that the bin could only be as wide as it was. It was just an oversight. If the bin isn't wide enough for something as common as a CD, what good is it? Nowadays we have to make sure that we design small holders and input jacks for Mp3 players and that we reserve enough flat space on the dashboard to accommodate GPS and satellite radio systems. These are the little things that people depend upon. Get them right, and people love their car and tell their friends to get one. Get them wrong, and people find their car to be frustrating and inconvenient.

If you pursue a career as an automotive interior designer you will never get the glory that will go to your colleagues in the exterior design department. Your efforts will have more effect upon long-term owner satisfaction, however, and a well-designed interior adds immeasurably to the overall package. It's where motorists spend most of their time."

I Am an Exterior Designer

"I have the job that everybody in this business wants. I am an automotive designer specializing in exterior design. I'm the person who puts dreams on paper and brings them to life.

It's never that easy, of course. I sketch wild flights of fancy every day knowing full well that most of them will never make it to the showroom floor. They're too esoteric, too hard to build, or just plain silly. The truth about cars is that most people only appreciate bold statements in other people's cars. Cars are fashion statements, and they go out of style. Most people want cars that will look good for as long as they want to drive them. They want flair, but not too extreme. They want to look up-to-date but not at the expense of looking out-of-date within a year or two. The market for truly stylish cars is actually very small.

Which makes an automotive designer's job much more challenging than you might think. Style must evolve but not as quickly as a true artist might prefer. My company's cars must all use a few of the same styling cues so that they can be easily differentiated from the competition. Some design hallmarks are associated with expensive cars, while others are associated with economy cars.

Every design has to function. Working with engineers can be rewarding or frustrating. We learn from each other. Sometimes their engineering improves by taking the time to compromise with my design. Sometimes my design is enhanced by accommodating their engineering requirements. It's a give-and-take process.

I've been in this profession ever since I graduated from college with a bachelor's degree in industrial design. I earned a master's degree early in my career in order to improve my skills and stay on the leading edge of design."

I Am Vice President of Design for a Large Auto Company

"I have spent all of my adult life in the auto business and I wouldn't trade it for anything. Cars aren't like most manufactured products. Cars reflect who we are, how we want to be perceived. They also affect other critical industries, like steel and oil.

I started my career as an industrial design major in college. My university offered a few courses in automobile design, and I took them all. I designed a range of cars as my senior project and explained how each one fit into a niche. I expanded my imaginary brand across several price points. My professors loved my designs and were also impressed that I took the market realities into consideration as I refined them.

I got my first job in the design department of a major American auto manufacturer. I went straight to Detroit, portfolio in hand. I could have started out just about anywhere, designing components or working as a design consultant to augment company design staffs. Since I knew I wanted to be the head of design someday, however, I figured I owed it to myself to go straight to the top.

I had my share of successes over the years. A few flops, too. Design is an artistic process. Mistakes are inevitable. If you're smart, you learn from them. In my opinion, this is the hardest part of the automotive design process. Cars are not like canvases. You can't just hide them in the closet after you've finished them. A mistake may be a good learning experience for a designer, but if it costs the designer's company millions of dollars it may not be so good for the designer's career.

As the VP of design, my job is to put together teams of designers who work well together. That can be very tricky. Visions often clash, and the artistic temperament can be unpredictable.

I always encourage designers to think about form first. This turns reality upside-down, because form doesn't mean much until function has been established. My belief is that it's always better to tone down a fantastic design to make it work than it is to add flair to something boring. Good designs are organic, with broad strokes and details flowing from one to another effortlessly. Adding flair usually means bolting on accessories that don't flow from anything. They always look like afterthoughts.

I love my job because I get to interpret the world around us and turn it into the objects of our dreams. It's not about sheet metal. It's about determining the contours of our lives."

I Am the Owner of a Sports Car Company

"Like many car nuts, I've been doodling and sketching cars all my life. I've owned dozens of them, modified them, raced them and even built them from scratch. I know everything there is to know about cars. So after a couple of decades working as a designer for a major manufacturer I pooled my resources with a few friends and started my own car company.

Ask most people to name car companies and they may come up with a dozen. Car buffs may continue naming to about 25 or 30, before they start to reach back to defunct outfits like Studebaker and Packard. What most people don't know is that there are hundreds of auto manufacturers in the world today, most of which produce anywhere from hundreds of cars a year to as few as a dozen. After five years in business we're in the middle of the pack. Our most ambitious plans don't call for building more than a thousand cars per year, ever.

Like all small manufacturers, we build specialty cars. There's no sense in trying to compete with multibillion-dollar global enterprises to build ordinary cars, so independents like us specialize in something, like luxury cars, off-road vehicles or sports cars. My company builds sports cars. They're extremely expensive and way, way cool.

We source most of our parts from other companies. We buy engines from a company in England, for example, and other parts from brand-name suppliers like Recaro, Brembo, Bilstein, Eaton and others. The only part you absolutely have to build yourself is the body.

We currently have two cars in production and I designed both of them. The small partnership that runs this company includes a few engineers, so we work together to make my designs functional. The designs include a fairly comfortable sports car that we can build as a coupe or a convertible, and a very aggressive and uncivilized sports car that we can build in street-legal and racing versions. The price tag on the least-expensive model starts in the six figures. These are not ordinary cars.

Most small manufacturers are labors of love that go broke in a few years. We're beating the odds so far, but this is a fickle business and we are competing against some of the deepest pockets in the world. The whole enterprise could go belly-up tomorrow. But you know what? I still have to pinch myself every morning because I can't believe how lucky I am to be building my own cars."

PERSONAL QUALIFICATIONS

ALMOST EVERYBODY HAS DOODLED and drawn cars. On napkins, in notebooks, during classes or meetings. They're one of the things we all fantasize about. Most of the cars we draw from our imagination look silly and would be impossible to build. To become a successful automotive designer you need artistic talent, passion for cars and a solid understanding of engineering.

Automotive designers have serious artistic talent backed up by years of training and experience. Designing cars is an art, just as painting and sculpture are. In fact, auto designers often sculpt designs out of clay before they build the real thing so that they can get an idea of how the finished product will look in reality, as opposed to a graphic on a computer screen. Designing something as complex as a car requires traditional artistic skills like sketching, and technical skills like facility with computer-aided design tools. It also requires innate talent. Judging the quality of details of design, like door handles, strakes or simple curves in sheet metal requires both experience and a knack that you are either born with or not. At your age you already know if you have the artistic talent necessary to succeed as an automotive designer.

Even if you have been endowed with artistic talent you will also need to love cars. Many people are passionate about cars – how they look, how fast they can go, how well they handle and any number of other factors. Your passion must be several degrees deeper. You need to be concerned about all of these attributes and more, but you also need to be concerned about the big picture. As a designer you will also need to consider factors like price points and competition both inside and outside your own company. A price point is the price target the company is aiming at during the design process. Cars at lower price points tend to be more utilitarian than cars at the higher end of the scale.

You must also gain a solid understanding of the engineering that goes into the cars you design. This makes industrial design different from most other arts. You will never be able to sit at your drawing table and dream up whatever you want. Form must always follow function. As a designer you should be able to avoid making unrealistic demands of the engineers who design the mechanical components that make cars go. Designers and engineers work together. If the plan is to create a car with a large engine, for example, designers need to know how to make room for it. If the plan calls for a convertible option, designers should know how to accommodate the extra bracing necessary to add torsional rigidity to the chassis. You don't need to become an engineer, but you do need to know enough to be able to collaborate with them.

ATTRACTIVE FEATURES

MILLIONS OF PEOPLE WOULD LOVE TO design their own cars. Only a few thousand get the privilege, and only a few dozen ever become well-known within the field. This imbalance between the number of auto designer jobs and the demand for them makes a career in automotive design a glamour profession, like acting or professional athletics. Success won't come easily, but when you've made it to the top you will definitely have accomplished something to be proud of. People who succeed in exciting professions are held in high esteem by those around them, and for good reason.

Designing automobiles is not like spending days behind an easel painting still-lifes. Automotive designers are artists, but they pursue their art in a very collaborative environment that includes engineers, accountants, marketing analysts and government regulators, among others. This may not sound conducive to letting your artistic passions run free, but nothing could be further from the truth. Realistic demands from collaborators inspire designers to craft their artistic visions in ways that enhance the practical aspects of the automobile. Your art will not stand on its own as a personal statement, but will actually help practical engineering to work better and be more appealing.

Automotive designers also get to work with the latest technologies, from computer-aided design systems, to assembly-line robots, to space-age tools and materials that allow designers more free reign than their predecessors ever dreamed possible. Modern cars can be curvy and stylish in ways that the cars of a few decades ago couldn't, because today's tooling can economically churn out complex parts in large numbers. New materials also lend themselves to new types of expression. Nobody in the 1950s, for example, seriously considered the possibilities offered by making cars out of plastic or carbon fiber. Both can be fashioned into shapes not possible with steel, and both save weight and cost.

UNATTRACTIVE FEATURES

THIS IS A SMALL PROFESSION, AND jobs aren't plentiful. Many people work in the industry, but only a few get to design entire cars. Even the designers at the top of the profession have to cobble together their final designs from many small designs supplied by parts designers all along in the process. Most of the people working in this career design small components of automobiles, like handles, latches, buttons, knobs, switches, facia and trim pieces, and all the other elements that make up a complete car. Only a handful of designers get to devise the master plans, the artist's renderings of what the finished car will look like. Those designers tend to get all the credit. A few even become famous, like Italy's Battista Farina, founder of the Pininfarina design firm, or Harley Earl, the first vice president of design at General Motors and the man behind such notable cars as the Cadillac Eldorado and Chevrolet Corvette. There's no reason you shouldn't aim for the top, but you should also be aware that the odds of getting there are small.

Many artists do not do well in collaborative environments. A stubborn insistence upon the superiority of one's own ideas is even a hallmark of the typical artist as a talented visionary determined to put his or her stamp on the project. If you're this kind of artist, automotive design is not a good career choice, nor is any kind of industrial design, for that matter. Industrial design is more akin to filmmaking, which is an utterly collaborative process that requires the creative talents of anywhere from a few dozen to a few thousand individuals. Industrial designers may get the credit for the final product, but along the way they have to adapt their vision to the needs of many others. You may be talented, but you may not have the right temperament for the process.

Industrial design can go very wrong. Art by committee often falls flat because it lacks the vigor of a single artist's passion. The collaborative nature of industrial design makes some degree of "groupthink" impossible to avoid, however, and the results can be less than inspiring. The Pontiac Aztek, the car voted the ugliest of all time in at least one poll, was the result of a drawn-out design process that involved numerous designers and even more competing influences from within Pontiac, including departments who wanted to try out new materials, marketing analysts aiming for a new niche and the ever-present accountants who wanted everybody to bring the project in at a target price. All cars are designed in essentially the same way, but in the Aztek's case the decentralization and lack of guidance got so far out of control that the company actually changed its rules for designing cars.

EDUCATION AND TRAINING

TO ENTER THIS PROFESSION YOU WILL need to earn a bachelor's degree in industrial design. This is a competitive, specialized profession. Majoring in something that seems like it would be closely related, like art or even automotive engineering, will not get you where you want to go. Industrial design is a separate field.

Industrial design applies artistic ideas to practical projects. A conventional work of art like a painting may evoke an emotional response, but such works of art don't have to *do* anything. Communicating emotion is their one and only function. Industrial design adds flair to function, often enhancing practicality in the process. The best examples of industrial design really are works of art that also work. Who has not gasped at the unexpected flash of a red Ferrari on a busy city street?

Many colleges and universities offer degrees in industrial design. Many art schools offer an associate degree program in industrial design, which may be a good option if you want to explore the profession without making a great commitment of time and money. If you want to become a full-time professional, however, you will need to earn a bachelor's degree and, ultimately, a master's degree.

A typical industrial design program consists of courses in model making, design methods, materials technology, manufacturing techniques and basic engineering. Industrial design majors also take courses that support the broader concept of industrial design, like art history, multimedia studies, cultural studies and sociology. The biggest part of the typical industrial design curriculum, however, is the studio. The "studio" in this context is a series of courses that may begin in the freshman year and continue until graduation, that require students to design industrial products on assignment. Under the guidance of department professors, students will design items of increasing complexity, some of which will become models and even working products manufactured in conjunction with students from the engineering department. The work you create in these studio classes will provide the foundation for your first portfolio of work to show to potential employers.

Some industrial design programs offer specialized courses in automotive design. Such courses may concentrate on interior or exterior design, while others teach students the finer points of items that most people never think about, like handles, switches and knobs. Before you scoff at taking a course in how to design a knob, think about the aftermarket knobs you've seen for sale in auto-parts stores. Some come in conventional shapes and feature logos from car companies and related products, while others hardly look like knobs at all. Obviously there is a market for distinctive knobs.

The best thing you can do to advance your skills during your college years is to complete an internship with a design studio or auto manufacturer. Most internships are paid and many come with special advantages not available to regular employees, like seminars and lectures devised specifically for interns. As an industrial design major you could find yourself working for an industrial design studio taking assignments from a wide array of clients. You may even get to work for a studio that handles automotive contracts. Either way, you will gain an inside view of the profession. You may get your first real job after college from a company you did an internship with.

You will probably have to earn a master's degree in industrial design if you want to stay competitive in this field. Many universities offer graduate programs in industrial design, often on a part-time basis so you can work during the day. A few universities offer specialized graduate programs in automotive design. However, you will be judged by the quality of your work, more than your degrees. Always keep copies of your best work.

EARNINGS

EARLY IN YOUR CAREER YOU CAN expect to earn from $45,000 to $65,000 per year. The actual figure will depend upon your employer, the region where you work and, most importantly, your performance. Salaries for industrial designers tend to top out between $100,000 and $150,000 for most designers. This figure does not include additional forms of compensation like stock awards, profit-sharing or bonuses, all of which may be paid to industrial designers. If you become the head of design for a major studio or auto manufacturer you can expect to earn much more.

Higher salaries come with management responsibilities. Your artistic inclination may lead you to concentrate only on grinding out new designs, but you can never forget that you will be a part of a large and complex organization that needs leaders to achieve its goals. After a few years as part of a team of designers you may find that you want the opportunity to help others to focus their efforts.

OPPORTUNITIES

THE AUTOMOTIVE DESIGN FIELD WILL always be a challenging profession to enter, but there are ways to triangulate on the career you want. You can never go wrong by improving your credentials. You will need a bachelor's degree to enter this profession but a master's degree will help you to get to the top. So will certificates earned along the way. Industrial design is an ever-changing field defined by technology, fashion and taste. Keeping abreast of developments within the field through additional education and training will help you to stay ahead of your competition. It will also help you to keep current with the marketplace. Fashions come and go and you don't want to be the designer who wasn't paying attention when fender skirts gave way to fender flares.

If the automotive design business doesn't get you where you want to go you can look into other sectors of industrial design. Your passion may be for cars, but what about motorcycles? Airplanes?

Military equipment? The field of industrial design is broad and deep, with plenty of opportunities if you are adaptable and enthusiastic. Many industrial designers work in several different fields during their careers, sometimes returning to favorite fields after spending a few years doing something else. The new perspective gained by designing different products often sheds new light on an old subject.

GETTING STARTED

YOU SHOULD ALREADY HAVE A pretty good idea of where you want to go and what you want to do by the time you graduate from college and start thinking about getting that first real job. Get your personal marketing materials in order. For an industrial designer, your portfolio is of utmost importance. Even if you are just out of college and none of your designs has actually been produced, your portfolio is the only means potential employers have to judge what you may be capable of. Gather together your best work and be prepared to present it in whatever format a potential employer wants. This may be in a traditional paper portfolio or via digital means, such as a video or PowerPoint presentation. Get some help from your teachers or friends in the industrial design department of your school to make sure you get it right.

Very few job openings are advertised. Most jobs are filled from within or by people who have some connection to the employer. It is very common for new graduates to get their first jobs with the companies where they did their internships because they are known to the employer and have a proven track record. Companies may even create a position for a former intern they really want to get back.

Look further afield, too. Talk to your teachers. Get in touch with friends who graduated a year or two ahead of you to find out what they're doing. Don't overlook job fairs. They may be crowded and confusing but you'll never find more employers all in one place.

No matter how your job search seems to be going, never lose faith in yourself. Your first job doesn't have to be your dream job. If it is, that's great. If it isn't, just do your best, keep copies of everything you do, add them to your portfolio and move along after a year or two. You'll learn valuable lessons along the way and be better equipped for the next opportunity.

ASSOCIATIONS
PERIODICALS
WEBSITES

■ **Alfa Romeo**
www.alfaromeo.com

■ **Arizona State University**
www.asu.edu

■ **Art Institutes**
www.artinstitutes.edu

■ **Aston Martin**
www.astonmartin.com

■ **Audi**
www.audiusa.com

■ **Automotive Design and Production**
www.autofieldguide.com

■ **Automotive News**
www.autonews.com

■ **AutoWeek**
www.autoweek.com

■ **Becker Automotive Design**
www.beckerautodesign.com

■ **BMW**
www.bmw.com

■ **California College of the Arts**
www.cca.edu

■ **Car and Driver**
www.caranddriver.com

■ **Car Body Design**
www.carbodydesign.com

■ **Car Design Online**
www.cardesignonline.com

■ **Car Design News**
www.cardesignnews.com

■ **Carnegie Mellon University**
www.cmu.edu

■ **Chrysler Corporation**
www.chrysler.com

■ **Classic and Sports Car**
www.classicandsportscar.com

■ **Concept Car Online**
www.conceptcaronline.com

■ **Core 77**
www.core77.com

■ **Ferrari**
www.ferrari.com

■ **Fiat**
www.fiat.com

■ **Ford Motor Company**
www.ford.com

■ **General Motors**
www.gm.com

■ **Industrial Designers Society of America**
www.idsa.org

■ **Industrial Design Served**
www.industrialdesignserved.com

■ **Jaguar**
www.jaguar.com

■ **Lamborghini**
www.lamborghini.com

■ **Lotus Cars**
www.grouplotus.com

■ **Mercedes-Benz**
www.mbusa.com

■ **Morgan Motor Company**
www.morgan-motor.co.uk

■ **Motor Trend**
www.motortrend.com

■ **Nissan**
www.nissanusa.com

■ **Product Design Forums**
www.productdesignforums.com

■ **Road and Track**
www.roadandtrack.com

■ **Rolls-Royce**
www.rolls-roycemotorcars.com

■ **Savannah College of Art and Design**
www.scad.edu

■ **Suzuki**
www.suzuki.com

■ **University of Washington**
www.washington.edu

■ **Volkswagen**
www.vw.com

■ **Yanko Design**
www.yankodesign.com